Please Be My
Hands

A BOOK ABOUT ASKING FOR HELP

Dr. Karen Hutchins Pirnot
ILLUSTRATIONS BY JULIE ROSS

the Peppertree Press
Sarasota, Florida

For information regarding permission,
call 941-922-2662 or contact us at our website:
www.peppertreepublishing.com or write to:
the Peppertree Press, LLC.
Attention: Publisher
1269 First Street, Suite 7
Sarasota, Florida 34236

ISBN: 978-1-61493-079-2

Library of Congress Number: 2011944008

Printed in the U.S.A.

Printed December 2011

Things do not change; we change.

Henry David Thoreau
1817-1862, *Walden*

Peter was very angry and he wanted to use his hands to punch at something. But, he couldn't make a fist; his hands didn't work anymore. He thought he might like to kick at a door to show how angry he was, but his feet didn't work either. Peter was one angry boy and he had been angry ever since that bad accident several months ago. The accident had put him in a wheelchair with a special mouth straw that helped the chair to move.

4

At first, Peter shouted his anger and that got him some attention. But now, no one seemed to notice the shouting. It seemed as if his shouting just wore everyone out. So Peter practiced getting a very good frown on his face. Hardly anyone paid any attention to the frown so that did him no good either.

6

One day, Peter's little sister Allie caught Peter frowning and she said, "Pete, you really need to turn that frown upside down." This made Peter even more angry and he glared at his little sister. Allie looked right at Peter's best glare and she said, "That doesn't look so hot either, Pete."

Allie did her best glare right back at Peter and it looked so silly that it surprised him. Then, he began to laugh. "I really don't look like that, do I, Allie?" he asked in between laughs.

"Yup! You look just like that, Pete," Allie answered truthfully.

8

Allie steered her brother to a mirror in the hallway and they both practiced their best eye glares and face frowns. They giggled until their stomachs hurt!

Finally, Peter said, "I think I'd better stop that, Allie. It's beginning to hurt. But I get so mad not being able to use my hands and my feet to do the things I want to do."

"Well, why didn't you say so, Pete?" Allie asked. "Just use my hands and my feet and ask me to do the things you want to do."

"You mean you would agree to be my hands and my feet now?" Peter asked with amazement.

"Sure, we all would, Pete. Just ask me or any of your friends and I bet you can use our hands and our feet just like you use our toys and our books and our time. But, Pete, you should be polite when you ask for a favor, you know," Allie reminded.

Peter smiled at his little sister and then he thought for a moment before asking, "Allie, please be my hands and get me a drink of water? Please?" he added quickly.

Allie smiled and immediately went to the kitchen, got a glass from the cupboard and ran some water from the faucet. She got a straw out of the drawer and put it into the glass. Then, Allie went to Peter and held the glass as she carefully placed the straw in his mouth. "Just the way you like it, right, Pete?" she asked.

"Perfect, Allie," Peter replied as he took a sip of the cool, fresh water. "Thanks for being my hands," he added with a smile.

"You did it, Pete!" Allie screamed with excitement.

"I did what?" Peter asked, confused.

"You turned that frown upside down, just like I asked!" Allie smiled.

Peter smiled for a moment and then said, "Allie, I could use a good pair of feet as well. Please, if you wouldn't mind," he added pleasantly.

"Sure, just name it, Pete. If I'm not busy, I'll be happy to lend you my feet," Allie smiled.

Peter moved his chair to the side door by sipping on the straw that moved his chair. "I'd like to go outside and see if I can find some feet to play ball with. But I need the door opened before I can go out," he said.

"So you need both my hands and my feet then, Pete. That's a pretty big favor but I think I can manage it," Allie said, going to the door and opening it wide so Peter's chair could move outside.

Allie and Peter went outside and soon, Peter's best friend Lenny came to join them. Peter told Lenny about how Allie had taught him to use other people's hands and feet in order to do the things he wanted to do and Lenny thought it was a great idea! He was more than willing to loan out his hands and his feet whenever he wasn't using them himself.

14

15

The three played kickball. At first, Peter would tell Lenny and Allie where to kick the ball. Then Peter had a great idea! He moved his chair to the end of the driveway so he could block the balls before they rolled into the street. He practiced until he could move his chair just right so that the ball would hit part of the chair and bounce back into the driveway. Pretty soon, he blocked every ball that came his way!

"You should be the goalie on the school team, Pete!" Lenny shouted.

Peter felt proud of his new wheelchair skills and he became more and more proud of what he could do. Before he knew it, there was no time to be angry about what he couldn't do.

"I wonder why I never thought to use your hands and feet before?" he asked his sister and his friend Lenny.

"You never asked, Pete," Allie said directly. "Our hands and feet have been here all along, but how were we supposed to know you wanted to use them?"

Peter smiled. "Well," he said, "now that I know I have hands and feet I can borrow, I'll be asking a lot."

"Good!" said Allie with her biggest Allie grin. "That makes me feel happy, Pete, 'cause sometimes, my hands and feet just have nothing to do and nowhere to go!"

16

Before long, Peter had so many people willing to help be his hands and feet that he became the busiest boy in town!

Other Books by Dr. Karen Hutchins Pirnot

*Designates award-winning books

Books available through Amazon.com and Barnes & Noble.com

For Teens and Adults:

Just a Common Lady*

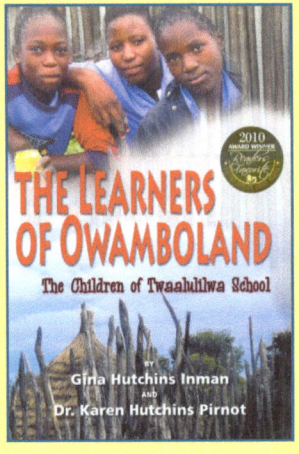

The Learners of Owamboland*

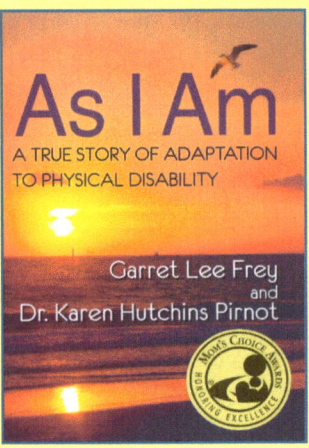

As I Am*

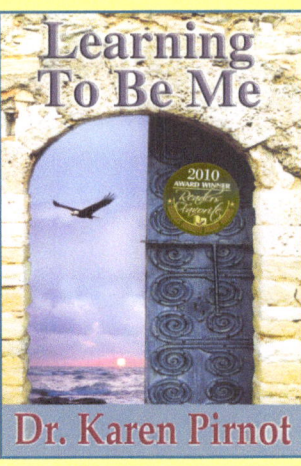

Learning To Be Me*

For Mothers and Grandmothers:

Keeper of the Lullabies*

To visit Dr. Pirnot or to order autographed books: www.drpirnotbooks.com